The Reflective Journal for

Researchers and Academics

Created by

Dr Jessica Taylor (FRSA)

Copyright © 2020 by VictimFocus (Dr Jessica Taylor)

All rights reserved. This book or any portion thereof may not be reproduced or used in any manner whatsoever without the express written permission of the publisher except for the use of brief quotations in a book review or scholarly journal with appropriate citation.

Book cover design by Johnson Marketing.

First Printing: January 2020

ISBN 978-0-244-23909-1

Dr Jessica Taylor T/A VictimFocus

Derby, UK

www.victimfocus.org.uk

Email: Jessica@victimfocus.org.uk

Ordering Information:

Special discounts are available on quantity purchases by corporations, associations, educators, and others. For details, contact the publisher at the above listed address.

This journal is dedicated to the researchers, students, academics and professionals who are committed to ethical research in social sciences and sensitive topics.

Our research means nothing if our methods and intentions are not ethical or reflective.

We must be willing to look at ourselves before we endeavor to look at others.

Contents

Section 1: Purpose and intentions of your research   8

Section 2: Your beliefs, values and perceptions of research   23

Section 3: Understanding your epistemological and ontological positions   45

Section 4: About your research participants   73

Section 5: Ethical considerations of your research   94

Section 6: Refining your research design and methodologies   120

Section 7: Reflecting on your findings and their impact on the real world   156

Section 8: Exploring the impact on self and your own experiences of conducting the research   179

Section 9: Scribbles, doodles and distractions   203

How to use this reflective journal

A foreword by Dr Jessica Taylor (PhD, FRSA)

Welcome to your new reflective research journal. You must be here because like me, you are interested in reflecting on your research journey. Research can be conducted as part of a university or college qualification, as part of our vocations or as part of our careers. No matter where you are designing or conducting research, you can use this journal to challenge yourself or your students.

I designed this journal with all of us in mind. We are all conducting sensitive, distressing and impactful research in many different disciplines. However, reflexivity is usually confined to qualitative researchers and academics. I would like this journal to encourage everyone to deeply reflect and question their own ethics, intentions, impact and methods.

Inside this journal are ten sections of reflection questions that are designed to help you think critically about your own values, practice, research design, analysis, real world impact and even the impact the research may have on you (personally or professionally).

You can use this journal however you like. There are over 230 pages of reflective tasks which include sentence completion, doodling, lists, questions and anecdotes. They are split into sections and each section begins with an explanation of the types of tasks that are included.

You may wish to use this journal once per day or once per week. It could be that you flick through the journal until you find a task that really jumps out at you or resonates with how you are feeling that day. Alternatively, you might decide to work methodically through this journal and complete one task per day until your research is completed. You could also read the contents page and then choose which section you want/need to complete. The choice is yours and this journal is private, confidential and personal to you.

You can shout, swear, challenge yourself, challenge the system, cry, celebrate and big yourself up in this journal. You can read a question and come back to it another day. You can choose to answer 10 questions in a day if you need to work on something that is bothering you.

The journal contains contentious, difficult, challenging, critical and interesting questions. It is for those who are ready to question themselves, to question the system and to question whether we are doing the best we can do for ourselves and for our research participants. Like most reflective tasks, you will get out of it what you put into it. If you choose not to dig deep or to be honest with yourself whilst answering the questions, you will only ever scratch the surface of the critical reflection you are truly capable of. However, if you are willing to use this journal as your personal space for self-reflection, learning and development – you are certain to gain a lot from this resource.

I hope you enjoy using this journal and the questions become part of your research process for many years to come. It is vital that we conduct impactful, ethical and progressive research for our participants. Without our participants, we have no research and we have no progress.

Thank you for committing to self-reflection and self-development.

SECTION 1

THE PURPOSE AND INTENTIONS OF YOUR RESEARCH

A section containing questions and tasks about the reasons why you are conducting your research and what you hope to achieve. Try to complete this section before any other section. Keep coming back to it as your research evolves, develops or takes you down different paths.

Use this section to help you to understand why you care about this research topic and what you want to achieve for yourself, for your participants or for the topic area.

1. List five reasons why you are interested in this topic area

2. What led you to this type of research?

3. What is your personal connection to this research and do other people know how you feel about it?

4. What do you want to gain from conducting this research project?

5. Write about what your participants would gain from your research – no matter what the findings might be

6. What would your research add to the current literature on this topic?

7. If you had to pick just one, which is the most important objective of your research project?

8. Write a newspaper headline and a short article for your research project

9. Explain your research project to a child who is asking about what you do

10. I don't want my research to…

11. How is your research going to be different from all the other research on this topic?

12. I would love my research to…

13. Think about the purpose and aims of your research. Who benefits most from your research and why?

14. How did you decide the aims of your research?

15. What do you intend to do with your research findings?

SECTION 2

YOUR BELIEFS, VALUES AND PERCEPTIONS

OF RESEARCH

This section contains tasks and critical thinking exercises designed to help you to consider your own beliefs, values and perceptions of research, your participants and your own role within the work.

Use this section to explore how you think and feel about people, approaches, research and purpose.

1. Write five reasons that research is conducted in your topic area.

1) After years of commentary on underrep in HE, it's still an unresolved issue

2) In terms of ethnic minorities; the group is evolving + changing etc. The issues that they face may be different to other ethnic groups (eg travellers / refugees)

3) Given the multi culturalism of England, there is still elitism that exists in HE, complex, entry into certain jobs.

4) W.P. activities have not worked. Funding in investment has been ineffective

5) Despite interventions + financial aid, underrep students are reluctant to enter HE. Why? Not belonging (due to elitism)

2. Research often reflects the interests of the researcher or institution. Discuss your thoughts on this statement.

- I am concerned with equality of opportunity especially for underrep students.
- Concern for them making informed choices + feel that very much depends on the IAG provision that exists within the instit that they attend. Whilst career practitioners cannot change structural inequalities that exist, we can provide as much iag for students so that they can make an informed decision about H.E.
- Making the right choice for underrep can be life changing for their future career + financial stability as well as fulfilment in career choice.

3. Give an example of research that has been conducted in your topic area that you do not feel was in the best interests of the participants

Maccabe (2021)

used 3 students + 9 staff @ Kingston Uni

↳ too narrow

↳ no news for im student.

4. The rules around research ethics can sometimes stop us from conducting important studies. Discuss this statement.

FOR

- Safeguards participants
- Forces researcher to consider what they are doing + why
- ↳ Questions / topic areas / sampling method etc

AGAINST

- Timing + admin reqd to fulfil ethics form.

5. Are there any theories or research conclusions in your topic area that you morally disagree with?

- Sweeping statement that underrep students have not entered HE because they are not as capable or that they are "unmotivated

- Belief that careers interventions do not work.

- Belief that students are negatively affected by their background.

6. Do the dominant theories in your research area need to be updated or amended for the modern day?

- Bourdieu's theory of habitus needs to be revised.

7. Do you feel that research participants in your discipline are treated with respect and dignity during research and write-up?

8. Think about unethical/harmful studies which are still considered to be influential or important. List some here and discuss your thoughts about their legacy.

9. What is your role as the researcher and how do you know whether your interpretations or conclusions are correct?

10. Write about three values or beliefs that you feel are incompatible with being a good researcher

11. Write a letter to your prospective participants about why you want to do this research and why they should trust you

12. One thing I would love to change about research in my topic area is…

13. If I had more influence in my field, I would change the way we talked about…

14. How can you ensure that your personal beliefs and values won't influence the way you conduct and interpret your research? Is it possible to do so?

15. Write about the way historic beliefs or values have influenced your topic area or discipline

16. Think about the theories and studies in your chosen topic area. What role has racism played in the methods, findings and interpretation?

17. Reflect on how far your discipline has come over the past 100 years. What beliefs and values have changed, and which have stayed the same?

18. Are there any beliefs or perceptions that are stopping the progress of your discipline or topic area?

19. What role has misogyny played in your topic area?

20. Are there any 'hidden' populations of participants who tend to be ignored or missed from research? Who are they and why are they unrepresented?

21. What do you think of the progress being made in your field of research? Is progress making a difference to people?

SECTION 3

UNDERSTANDING YOUR EPISTEMOLOGICAL AND ONTOLOGICAL POSITIONS

This section contains tasks and questions that will help you to explore and understand your own philosophical positions in your research.

Many students and academics are intimidated by the concepts and language of epistemology and ontology. However, they are easy to work through with some simple questions about the world and knowledge of the world.

This section has been designed with thinking and writing tasks to explore your own philosophical positions and why you think you hold them. However, there are also some knowledge-based tasks here that may require some research to answer (if you don't already know the answers).

1. Ontology is the theory of the nature of reality. What is reality and what is not? How do we know what reality is?

Some people argue that ontological views exist on a spectrum between realism and anti-realism – and that all theories of ontology can be broadly divided into realism and anti-realism (often, relativism).

A realist accepts that objects, facts and items exist independently of the human mind whereas an anti-realist argues that 'reality' and all of its objects, facts and items are subjective based on the perceptions and capabilities human mind.

Where do you see yourself as a researcher?

2. Think and write about the following statement: We build our own reality based on our personal experiences.

3. Relativists argue that reality is completely based on the human cultural, historical and personal perception and reference. What do you think of this position?

4. What would happen to the world if we adopted a pure realist position?

5. What is more important to you as a researcher; the establishment and acceptance/rejection of objective facts about the participants; or the exploration of the perceptions and beliefs constructed by the participants?

6. How much of your research topic area is based on relativism?

7. Do any of the authors/studies you have read expressly state their ontological position? If not, how can you work out their philosophical approach?

8. How confident are you about your own ontological position and how did you come to your decision?

9. Are there any ontological positions that you feel would be unhelpful in your topic area? If so, why?

10. Write about the ontological position that makes you the most uncomfortable and why.

11. Why is your ontological position important to your research?

12. Where do you think you sit between realism and relativism? Do you lean towards one more than the other? Why?

13. Critical realism is an ontological position between realism and relativism. Key theorists argued that there are facts and concepts of reality that exist regardless of how or whether we perceive them – but there are also 'facts' and concepts that are relative to the culture, history and personal experience of the human. What do you think of this approach?

14. Epistemology is the theory of knowledge and how we come to know what we know. When it comes to 'knowledge' about the world, epistemology explores whether we can know something or not and whether it is subjective or objective knowledge.

    There are many epistemological positions which sit on the ontological spectrum between realism and relativism. If you have already considered and decided upon your ontological position, you now need to consider the epistemology of your research.

    Epistemology is a vast field and includes positions such as constructivism, rationalism, idealism, empiricism

    Where do you see yourself as a researcher?

15. Are all issues in society socially constructed?

16. List five facts, objects or concepts in the world that exist outside of the mind of humans, and will continue to exist even if humans constructed them to be different or non-existent

17. Does language construct everything around us? How does this perspective influence your own topic area?

18. Think about the positivist argument that only observable phenomena can provide credible data or facts. How would this epistemological approach help or hinder your own research?

19. Write about how your chosen research methods align with your epistemological position

20. Consider what the best research methods would be if you were to adopt a social constructionist view in your research

21. Are there any epistemological approaches that you prefer? Why do you think that is?

22. To what extent do you agree that the epistemological position is the foundation of the entire research project, methods and findings?

23. If all things are socially constructed using language, couldn't language be used against the participants or researchers to argue that there is no 'issue' or that the issue only exists because it is constructed that way?

24. Interpretivism argued that the research methods we use in natural science cannot be applied to social science. Instead, we need to understand that all interpretations are culturally, historically and personally defined. What is your opinion?

25. Critical theory argues that the primary purpose of research is to change situations for real people and real-world issues. How does this apply to your own research topic?

26. Feminist epistemology starts from the position that the world is patriarchal and that women are oppressed. Discuss how this could play a role in your own research topic.

27. How are power structures impacting your own research topic and how does your epistemology account for them?

SECTION 4

ABOUT YOUR RESEARCH PARTICIPANTS

This section contains tasks and questions about your participants, their agency, their voice and their role in your research.

Use this section when you want to consider who your participants are and why you are engaging them in your research project.

1. Write about your research participants. Who are they and what do they have in common?

2. Write about why you chose to focus on your chosen sample of participants.

3. Imagine that you are challenged by another academic who tells you that you should have included other people in your sample. Use this space to tell them why you chose your sample and why you excluded others from this project.

4. What are the rights of your participants and how are you going to uphold them during and after your research?

5. If you were taking part in your own study, what would you be worried about as a participant?

6. Are your participants usually overlooked or misrepresented? How will you ensure that your own work effectively represents their views and experiences?

7. Write about the power dynamic between you and your participants.

8. How are you going to ensure that your interpretation of the participants' data is correct?

9. Plan how you will make sure that your participants can read your finished research project in an accessible and ethical way

10. How will you protect your participants from becoming distressed or harmed by your research?

11. Are your participants fully informed about the nature of your research? Why/why not?

12. Out of respect for your participants and their experiences, which terms, language or phrases will you avoid when talking or writing about your research topic?

13. How can you be sure that your participants feel comfortable enough to tell the truth about their experiences?

14. How can you recruit your participants in an ethical and effective way?

15. How will your honour your participants in your final report, presentation or write-up?

16. If you had to make a decision to only focus on one group of participants in your research, how and why did you make that decision?

17. How will you support participants who speak other languages or speak English as a second language?

18. When it comes to your participants, consider the difference between anonymity and confidentiality. Which one can you offer to your participants and how will you do it?

19. Consider the needs and rights of your participants and write them all down on this page. How will you ensure that your research project protects their rights and supports their needs?

20. How important is a diverse sample of participants in your research project? Why?

SECTION 5

ETHICAL CONSIDERATIONS OF YOUR RESEARCH

This section contains questions and tasks to support your thinking about ethical, effective research which respects your participants.

Use this section to learn more about your ethical considerations, approaches and concerns. This section may be useful to complete before you write an ethics application for your research project.

1. How will your research benefit your participants?

2. Write down all of the ways your participants could be harmed, distressed or upset by your research

3. What are the consequences of conducting unethical research with your participants?

4. In your topic area, what do you consider to be 'ethical' research and what do you consider to be 'unethical' research?

5. Are there any common practices, methods or theories in your field that you consider to be unethical? Write about them here.

6. How do you know that you are not exploiting your participants?

7. Do you believe that you benefit from this research project? In contrast, how do your participants benefit from taking part and giving you their data?

8. How can you protect the data of your participants in this research project?

9. Do you consider yourself to be in a power dynamic with your participants? How are you going to manage it?

10. Write about how you will deal with a disclosure from a participant and how it might make you feel.

11. If you were concerned about the responses from a participant, how would you safeguard them from harm?

12. Do you think that your discipline or field is ethical when it comes to human research?

13. How will your participants be able to withdraw their responses (a) during the study and (b) after the study?

14. How will you create an opportunity so that your participants can correct you if your interpretation of their data is wrong?

15. Is your research with vulnerable people or children? How will your research benefit those participants?

16. If your research will not directly benefit the participants of the study, why should they take part?

17. Are there any theories or approaches to your research project that could offend or harm your participants?

18. Is deception necessary in your research project? If it is, consider why. If it is not, consider if you feel deception is ever necessary in human research.

19. How will you support participants who are discussing or submitting data about sensitive topics?

20. Write a list of ethical pledges to your participants that you will adhere to throughout your research project

21. How do you plan to share your research findings in an accessible and ethical way?

22. How will you deal with data, transcripts or responses which contain offensive language or comments?

23. Consider whether your discipline has the power to oppress groups of people or participants. How will you ensure you do not collude with this oppression?

24. How important is ethics to you as a researcher?

25. Do you believe that you can be 'equal' to your research participants and there be no power imbalance present?

SECTION 6

REFINING YOUR RESEARCH DESIGN AND METHODOLOGIES

This section is about your research design, methods and approaches. It contains questions about why you have chosen your research design and how you feel it will benefit the research, the participants and the understanding of the topic.

Use this section when you want to explore the best research methods for your topic.

1. How do you know which methods are best for this research project?

2. Write down three different methodological approaches that are often taken when conducting studies similar to your own

3. What is the most dominant research method in your topic area and why?

4. Draw a grid across this page to make four boxes. In each box, write about four key studies that relate to your project and what their methodologies were.

5. Considering your ontology and epistemology, what methods do you think would work best in this project and why?

6. Which methods are inappropriate for your research project and why are you ruling them out?

7. How will you recruit your participants? Make a list of how you will do it and what materials you will need.

8. What kind of study design have you chosen and how did you come to that decision?

9. What are your thoughts on using mixed methods for this research project? Could it strengthen your evidence?

10. What are your thoughts on using a qualitative approach to this project?

11. What are your thoughts on using a quantitative approach to this project?

12. If you are thinking of using a questionnaire, try designing some of your items and their item responses here

13. How will you collect data and why is it the best method of collection for your project?

14. How will you store your data safely and when will you delete it?

15. Write three different ways you could analyse your data and then number them in order of preference

16. What is the most effective way to present your findings?

17. Use this space to talk about methods of analysis you would like to use but don't know much about

18. Imagine you could run your study three times using three different methods of data analysis to explore different features of the data. Write the three methods here and how you would use them.

19. Write about a method of data analysis that is common in this topic area, but you don't want to use in your own project

20. How will you ensure that your findings are accurately representing the issues or experiences of the participants?

21. What research method skills or knowledge do you feel you lack for this research project? Is there anything you need more training/reading on before using?

22. Which pieces of software do you need for your research methods or data analysis methods?

23. If resources or time were not an issue, what research design and data analysis method would you choose for this study?

24. How would you design a longitudinal study in your topic area and what do you think it would find?

25. If you are using questionnaire items, write here about how the phrasing or words of your items might change the answers that your participants give

26. How will you account for or reduce socially desirable responses in your data?

27. Do you need to consider practice effect or repetition in your study? Will this impact your findings or validity?

28. How can you make sure your study is reliable and valid?

29. Have you considered how ecologically valid your study is? How can you make your research as valid as possible?

30. What are the confounding variables you might need to consider?

31. How do the dominant theories compliment your chosen research methods?

32. Is your study too long or boring for the participants?

33. Are you offering a reward for taking part in your study? How can you be sure that you are not exploiting people who need that reward (money, vouchers, access to services)?

34. How will you deal with missing data and why?

35. Is it always ethical to fill in missing data using statistical software?

SECTION 7

REFLECTING ON YOUR FINDINGS AND THEIR IMPACT IN THE REAL WORLD

This section contains questions and thinking tasks that encourage you to explore and reflect on your research findings. Further, the tasks support you to consider what the implications are for future research, the participant group, the community, wider social issues and 'real world' problems.

Use this section when you want to work through your findings to seek meaning, purpose, impact and context.

1. How are you feeling about your findings?

2. In hindsight, did you go into this project hoping for a particular set of findings? Has this had any impact on you or the study?

3. Write about one of your findings that surprised you and why

4. Do you think your interpretation of the findings is accurate? How do you know?

5. What do your findings mean to you?

6. If you presented your findings to your participants as raw data, what do you think they would say?

7. How do the dominant theories relate to your findings?

8. Do any of your findings contradict established theories or arguments?

9. What impact will your findings have on participants?

10. Are there any findings that you would be nervous about showing to your participants or target group?

11. If you have any controversial or contentious findings, write about them here.

12. Write three key findings from your project and why they are important to the topic area

13. Which theories or authors are confirmed or supported by your findings?

14. Would your findings change with a different sample (larger, mixed, different region, age group etc.)?

15. How will you talk about your findings as important without generalizing or extrapolating?

16. What is the 'story' of your findings and research? What message do you want to convey?

17. Could your participants read your findings before you submit or publish, to get their thoughts or to check your interpretations?

18. How could your findings change the world for your participants?

19. How could your findings impact future research?

20. If you planned another research project to build upon your findings, what would you explore next?

21. How can you publish your findings so that they don't end up behind a paywall?

22. How can you share your findings so that the people who need it most, can access the information and learning they need?

SECTION 8

EXPLORING THE IMPACT ON SELF AND YOUR OWN EXPERIENCES OF CONDUCTING THE RESEARCH

This section provides space for you to explore your own experiences, personal views and impact during the research process.

Use this section when you would like to explore the impact on yourself.

1. Do you have any personal connection or interest to the research topic?

2. Do any aspects of your research make you nervous?

3. How has working in this topic area changed the way you think?

4. What do you think the personal impact of this research has been on you?

5. Do you feel supported whilst you conduct this research?

6. Did any of your reading make you uncomfortable? What was it and why do you think it made you feel like that?

7. Write about why you have a passion for this topic

8. How has your worldview changed throughout this topic?

9. One thing I feel I need to learn more about is…

10. Write about a study in your field of work that changed the way you thought about an issue

11. Is it really possible to 'leave your own stuff at the door' and to be completely objective in your research?

12. Are you getting enough psychological and practical support during this research project? What do you need more or less of?

13. How have your life experiences influenced the direction of your research?

14. Would you prefer to have all the knowledge of your topic that you have now, and be aware – or have none of that knowledge and be oblivious?

15. My favourite theory in my line of work is…

16. How stressful has this project been and how have you coped?

17. How has this research changed you as a person or as a researcher?

18. Write about the aspect of your research that is worrying you. List all your worries here.

19. Do you think there will come a time when you need to stop doing this kind of research and move on to another topic area?

20. How has your research supervision been?

21. You are given a £300 budget to spend on research expenses or development. What do you spend it on?

22. We are at our most dangerous when we assume that we know all there is to know about our topic. Discuss this perspective.

23. Write about some literature you read that had a personal impact on you.

SECTION 9

MY NOTES AND IDEAS

This section contains space to explore and record your own ideas, notes, findings, theories and models as you work through your research project.

Ideas for new research projects

Theories I love and theories I hate

Reminding myself why I am doing this project...

My ideas about my findings

Mind mapping stuff

Doodle your research topic

The title of my book or paper would be…

Create a timeline for your research

Draw the person who inspires you to be a better researcher

Draw yourself. With a huge cup of coffee. The cup has to be bigger than your head.

My models

My models

Creating my own theory

# Creating my own theory

Notes page

Notes page

Notes page

Eek! You finished your research journal!

How do you feel?

What to do now:

- Read back through your journal and consider if any of your answers have changed over the months
- Consider which questions you didn't answer or struggled to answer
- Use your journal to write up your papers, chapters or books
- Consider whether you want to keep this journal full of your ideas, thoughts and feelings… or kill it with fire
- Buy another journal for the next project, obviously
- Tell loads of people that they need a copy of this journal
- Start planning all the other research you want to do next
- Consider how you can share your research findings as widely as possible for free
- Carry on being reflective, critical and ready to learn
- Continue to change the world, one research project at a time
- Pour a gin, mate

- Bryman's social research methods
  Tom Clark Liam Foster.

- Denscombe 2017. (social research).
  (Quantative)

- Shay sessions.
- Moustakas CE 2013. — library
  Mustafkas - methodology. ─────
     ↳ phenomenological research methods.

Printed in Great Britain
by Amazon

76068045R00127